OUR COMMUNITY™

Let's Visit the Police Station

Marianne Johnston

WITHDRAWAL

The Rosen Publishing Group's
PowerKids Press™
New York

Published in 2000 by The Rosen Publishing Group, Inc.
29 East 21st Street, New York, NY 10010

First Edition

Book design: Danielle Primiceri

Photo Credits: p. 4 © Ralph Morang/New England Stock Photography; pp. 7, 8, 20 © Mark Reinstein/ Uniphoto Picture Agency; p. 11A Phyllis Picardi/International Stock; p. 11B © Laura Dwight/CORBIS; p. 12 © Tom Carroll/International Stock; p. 15A © Frank Siteman/New England Stock Photography; p. 15B © Ron Chapple/FPG International; p. 15C L. O'Shaughnessy/New England Stock Photography; p. 16 © Kim Karpeles/New England Stock Photography; p. 19 © Dick Luria/FPG International.

Johnston, Marianne
        Let's visit the police station / by Marianne Johnston.
            p.   cm. — (Our community)
        Summary: A simple introduction to the role of the police in a community, describing the work they do, what goes on in a station, the equipment used, and various types of police officers.
        ISBN 0-8239-5434-X (lib. bdg.)
        1. Police Juvenile literature. 2. Police stations Juvenile literature. [1. Police. 2. Police stations.] I. Title. II. Series: Johnston, Marianne. Our community.
        HV7922.J65   1999
        363.2—dc21   99-21296
                                                                                                    CIP

Manufactured in the United States of America

Contents

History of the Police

Police as we know them today have not been around that long. In the 1700s, watchmen were hired by cities like Boston and New York to keep an eye out for criminals.

In 1845, New York became the first city in America to have an organized police department. The city had a police station that served as a home base for all of its officers, and they had a full staff of police whose job it was to make sure that everyone in the **community** followed the laws. Today almost every community has a police station.

◄ *The police help to keep the community safe.*

At the Police Station

The first thing you see as you enter the police station is usually the police desk. The officers behind the police desk are the ones to go to if you have a question or need to report a crime. Most police stations have a small waiting area where people can wait to file a report or for relatives of people who have been **arrested**. Police stations often have holding cells, or places where they keep people for a short time after they have been arrested. Police stations usually have locker rooms with lockers for the officers' uniforms.

The police have to work together to solve problems in the community. ▶

Captains and Platoons

Police officers are divided into groups called platoons. In an average city, each platoon has about 50 officers. A captain is put in charge of each platoon. At the beginning of every shift, the captain meets with his platoon in the **roll call room**. The captain checks to make sure that everyone is there, assigns officers to cases, and passes along any information about criminals on the loose that the officers should know about.

◄ *This police captain is doing the roll call for his platoon.*

Communications Center

When you call 911 or the emergency number for your area, an operator will answer your call and ask you what the emergency is. If you need a police officer, the operator types your address and the problem into a computer. The operator then sends your information from her computer to the **police dispatcher's** computer. In some cities, the operator and the police dispatcher are in one room. This room is called a communications center. In other cities, the operator and the police dispatcher are in separate buildings.

When you have an emergency, you should call the emergency number and talk to the operator. ▶

The Police Dispatcher

The police dispatcher sits at a desk with several computer screens in front of her. She wears a headset that is attached to a radio. When the operator calls, the address of the problem pops up on her computer screen. The computer tells her which police officers are assigned to that area. She reads the code number of the closest officer and the location of the problem into the headset. The headset sends her voice out over the radio. When an officer hears his number, he tries to get there as fast as he can to help with the emergency.

The dispatcher reads the address of the problem into her headset so the police know where to go.

Different Types of Police Officers

All police officers must spend about six months at the Police Academy. They learn how to handle a gun and how to drive a car in a high-speed chase. They also learn about how to arrest someone. Once they are out of the academy, there are many different jobs police officers can have. Some are traffic cops, who make sure people are obeying traffic laws such as driving under the speed limits and stopping at stop signs. There are also **detectives**, who try to figure out who committed a crime.

Some police work with dogs, who use their great sense of smell to sniff out drugs and weapons. ▶

Patrol Officers

The police you see around your community are probably patrol officers. Their main job is to be out in the community, either on foot or in cars, stopping crime. Patrol officers carry many items that they may need to use when dealing with criminals. They carry **handcuffs** in case they need to arrest someone. They carry a flashlight, a stick called a **baton**, and sometimes **pepper spray** to help defend themselves. They carry a gun, too, in case they must protect themselves or someone else from a dangerous criminal.

◀ *Patrol officers also carry radios, so they can hear the dispatcher's calls.*

The Patrol Car

There are a lot of **gadgets** inside the patrol car that the police can use to get the attention of other drivers or of criminals. There is a black panel with buttons on it between the two front seats. These buttons control the sirens and the lights on top of the car. The officer can also press a button so that his voice can be heard through a speaker on the top of the car. Besides the flashing lights on top of the car, patrol cars also have bright spotlights on the sides of the car so that an officer can see what is going on down a dark alley or street.

This police car uses its blinking lights ▶
to move quickly through traffic.

How Computers Help the Police

Computers are very important to the police because they help spread information about a crime quickly. In some cities, each patrol car has its own computer. When an officer stops someone for breaking a law, he can type the person's name into his patrol car computer. If this person has committed a crime in the past, this crime will show up on the computer. Police dispatchers will sometimes send non-emergency calls, like a complaint about a barking dog, directly to the officer's patrol car computer instead of calling them out over the radio.

◄ *There is a lot of technology inside the patrol car.*

Community Policing

Police officers are some of the most important people in our communities. They make sure that everyone obeys the laws, so we can all be safe. Police officers also sometimes teach classes in the community about personal safety and drug prevention. Officers visit schools to talk to kids about staying safe. Being involved in communities helps police officers keep communities safe.

Web Sites:

You can learn more about the police on the Internet. Check out this Web site:

22 http://www.askacop.com

Glossary

arrested (uh-REST-ed) When someone is taken back to the police station because a police officer has reason to believe he broke the law.

baton (buh-TAHN) A black stick strapped to a police officer's belt used for self-defense when dealing with a dangerous criminal.

community (kuh-MYOO-nih-tee) A group of people who have something in common, such as a special interest or the area where they live.

detectives (dee-TEK-tivz) People who work for the police department and have the job of figuring out who committed crimes.

gadgets (GA-jets) Small tools designed to do a certain task.

handcuffs (HAND KUFS) Two steel rings joined by a short chain and locked around the wrists of an arrested person.

pepper spray (PEP-er SPRAY) A chemical sprayed into a criminal's eyes, used in self-defense.

police dispatcher (po-LEES DIS-patch-er) The person at the central police department who routes emergency calls to individual patrol officers.

roll call room (ROHL KAHL ROOM) A room in the police station where the patrol officers gather before every shift to get information and instructions from their captain.

Index